Shopping
In Grandma's Day

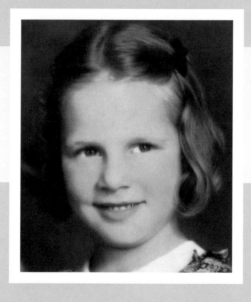

by Valerie Weber
and Beverly Crawford

Carolrhoda Books, Inc./Minneapolis

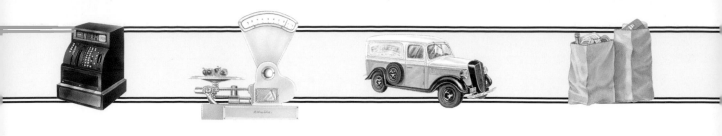

Carolrhoda Books, Inc., A Division of the Lerner Publishing Group
241 First Avenue North, Minneapolis, MN 55401 U.S.A.

Website address: www.lernerbooks.com

Planning and production by Discovery Books
Edited by Faye Gardner
Text designed by Ian Winton
Illustrations by Stuart Lafford
Commissioned photography by Sabine Beaupré and Jim Wend

The publishers would like to thank Beverly Crawford and Charlotte Slater for their help
in the preparation of this book.

Library of Congress Cataloging-in-Publication Data

Weber, Valerie.
    Shopping in grandma's day / Valerie Weber and Beverly Crawford ; [illustrations by Stuart Lafford].
      p.   cm. — (In grandma's day)
    Includes index.
    Summary: Recalls what it was like to help out in the family grocery store and to go shopping in Milwaukee, Wisconsin, during the 1940s.
    ISBN 1-57505-324-1 (alk. paper)
    1. United States—Social life and customs—1945 1970—Juvenile literature. 2. Shopping—United States—History—20th century—Juvenile literature. 3. Milwaukee (Wis.)—Social life and customs—Juvenile literature. 4. Shopping—Wisconsin—Milwaukee—History—20th century—Juvenile literature. 5. Crawford, Beverly, 1934-   —Childhood and youth—Juvenile literature. [1. Shopping—History—20th century. 2. Grocery trade—History—20th century. 3. Crawford, Beverly, 1934–   —Childhood and youth.] I. Crawford, Beverly, 1934–   . II. Lafford, Stuart, ill. III. Title. IV. Series: Weber, Valerie. In grandma's day.
E169.02.W39 1999
977.5'95043—dc21   98-12280

Printed in Hong Kong
Bound in the United States of America
1 2 3 4 5 6 - OS - 04 03 02 01 00 99

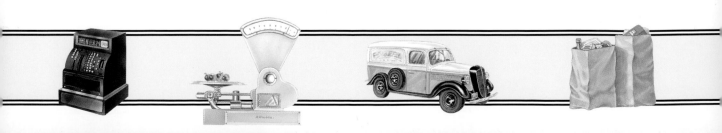

Contents

My name is Beverly Crawford. I have two grandchildren, Sarah, who is six, and Noah, who is eight. I was born in 1934 and grew up in Milwaukee, Wisconsin, with my parents and my little sister, Sandy.

This is a photograph of Sandy and me when I was six and she was three.

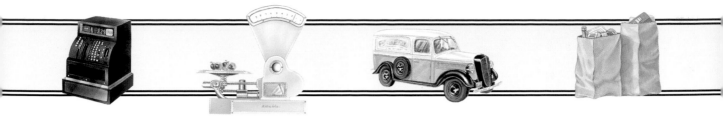

I lived with my family in a duplex, similar to the one shown in the photograph below. Lots of my relatives lived nearby, so there were always other children to play with.

My father owned a grocery store. Stores were different in the 1940s, when I grew up, and so was shopping. I'd like to tell you how my family and other families shopped during that time.

My Parents' Store

My mother and father's grocery store was a real family business. It provided many of my relatives with jobs. The photograph below shows how the store looked. You can see my father and mother working behind the meat counter. This photo was taken before I was born.

Lots of other family members worked as sales clerks in the store, including my aunt Nettie and several cousins. You can see my aunt Nettie in the photo above. She is the woman on the right. The woman in the middle is named Mary, and the woman on the left is named Jean. Jean and Mary weren't relatives, but they both worked in the store, too.

As I grew older, I also got to work in the store. The photo on the left was taken when I was fourteen years old. I felt so important wearing that white apron and serving customers.

Stores When I Grew Up

My father's grocery store looked like most others. Fruits and vegetables lay in bins in the front window, and a long counter with a cash register and scales on it ran along the side wall. Display cases had separate bins with glass fronts. Flour, sugar, beans, and even cookies filled each bin. Most things were sold in bulk, right out of the bins, rather than in individual packages. People just asked for the exact amount of anything they needed.

Instead of customers looking through the store aisles for what they wanted, a store clerk would get each item for each person. When I became a clerk at age twelve, I sliced meats and cheeses on a big slicing machine and wrapped them in waxed paper for customers. I also measured out flour, sugar, and potatoes into the store's paper bags. (Plastic bags hadn't been invented yet.)

Shopping for Food

Families did a little shopping every day because most people didn't have a refrigerator to keep food cold. Instead, they had iceboxes like the one below. Iceboxes were kept cold by huge chunks of ice delivered by truck. Frozen foods were uncommon, and most families bought canned fruits and vegetables if they couldn't get fresh ones.

There were few supermarkets at that time. Instead, most neighborhoods had lots of small stores. There was usually a grocery store, a fish store, a bakery, and a butcher shop that sold fresh meat.

People did their shopping by walking from one shop to the other until they had everything they needed. Shopping took longer then, but it was also more

interesting, since we got to talk to all of the shopkeepers.

I liked the butcher shop, where the staff wore aprons and caps and the smell of the sawdust on the floor filled the air. In the window hung chickens, geese, and ducks on hooks. They still had their heads, but their feathers had been plucked.

Shopping for Clothes and Hardware

Most people had less money in those days. People made their own clothes and had their shoes fixed by the local cobbler, rather than buying new ones. Most neighborhoods had a tailor shop, too. On the corner of my block stood a dry goods store, where people could buy clothing and fabric. How I loved going with my mom to pick out a piece of fabric for a new dress. I spent ages choosing from the rolls of cloth stacked on the long wooden counters.

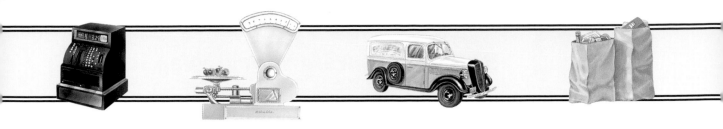

Next to the dry goods store was the hardware store, which stocked all kinds of household equipment and electrical goods. The front windows were cluttered with fireplace equipment, and garden tools hung from wires.

Most of the small stores were open until seven or eight o'clock every day but closed on Sunday. My family's store stayed open on Sunday, too.

Rationing during World War II

From 1941 until 1945, the United States fought in World War II in Europe and Asia. Because the armed forces needed food, weapons, and other supplies to help win the war, certain items were rationed in the United States.

Rationing meant that families could not always get as much as they wanted of some things. To control how much of these items families bought, the government gave out ration coupon books. If a family had the money and the ration coupons, they could buy four ounces of butter and twenty-eight ounces of meat or other protein foods each week. Every two weeks, a family could buy a pound of sugar.

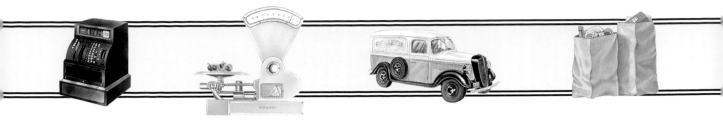

Rationing sometimes meant we had to wait in line for hours. Certain goods, like nylon stockings, butter, and sugar, were scarce. Shopping for them could take a whole morning. My mom used to leave me in the line for stockings while she went off to do other shopping.

Going Downtown

My mom and I sometimes took the bus or the streetcar downtown to go shopping. It seemed like the buses were always crowded. I usually stood on the bus, holding on to a strap. You had to pull a cord to ring the bell for your stop. A one-way bus ride cost ten cents for children under twelve.

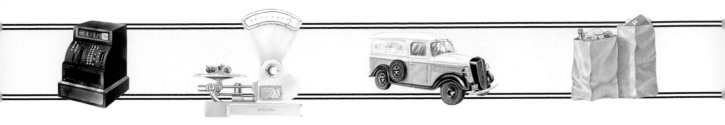

Going downtown was very exciting. The streets were busy and noisy with traffic, and the buildings seemed huge compared to those in my neighborhood. The photo below shows what downtown Milwaukee looked like back then.

In those days, there were no malls with lots of different stores all together in one building. We often went to a large department store, like Gimbels or Schuster's, or to smaller shops, such as Florsheim Shoes or Lawtons Clothes Store. (You can see Gimbels on the left side of the street in the photograph.) Those stores aren't around anymore.

Shoe Stores

Shopping for shoes was really exciting. Each year, I got one pair of shoes for school and one pair of dress shoes. In those days, you could get a pair of leather shoes for $3.98!

Sometimes the shoe store clerk put my feet in an X-ray machine to find my shoe size. It was fun to see the bones in my feet. We've since learned that too many

X rays are not good for you and that you should only have your foot X-rayed if something is wrong with it.

My doctor told my mother that my feet were flat so I had to wear special shoes. I thought my brown oxford shoes were so ugly! I wanted shiny, black patent leather shoes like my friends wore.

Shoes back then had leather soles, instead of rubber or plastic soles like you might have. When the soles on my shoes wore out, we visited the cobbler.

The cobbler fitted each shoe upside down on a metal mold and put a flat piece of leather on the sole. Then he hammered thin nails into the leather, before trimming off all the extra leather with a sharp knife. And I had a new sole!

Department Store Adventures

If an aunt or a cousin took me shopping as a treat, we usually went downtown to Schuster's department store. Once inside the big doors, I could smell the rich aroma of the delicious chocolates at the candy counter. We passed the counter on our way to the elevator at the back of the store.

At each floor, the elevator operator called out the number and what was sold on that floor. "Fourth floor, ladies' clothes and purses." I remember once, as the doors opened, I saw many women crowding around tables of leather purses.

Leather was scarce during the war, and those women had had to wait a long time to buy new purses. I was surprised to see such a crowd.

We often stayed on the elevator all the way to the seventh floor. There we might have lunch in the store restaurant and watch a fashion show. I felt so grown-up. And best of all, we always had hot fudge sundaes for dessert.

Shopping for Treats

I also liked shopping with friends. Our big treat was to go into dime stores like Woolworth's, Kresge's, or Grant. Sometimes my parents would give me a dime to spend. A dime could buy a lot in those days.

I liked to spend my money on candy. Some of the candy was the same as you might buy, but the prices were different. Hershey's Kisses cost one penny each, and most candy bars, like Hershey's, Three Musketeers, and Baby Ruths, were a nickel.

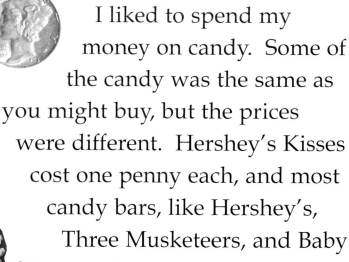

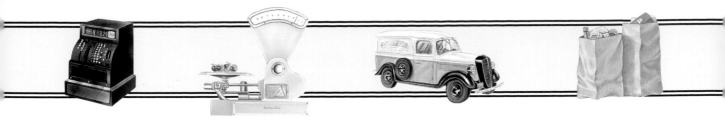

Everything was much cheaper back then. You could get a two-gallon fish tank for forty-nine cents. Guppies or snails for that tank cost five cents each. Fifty cents could get you a new baby doll or five different comic books. I always wanted a talking doll, but they cost a lot of money— almost six dollars!

Street Vendors

Sometimes shopping came to us. In the summer, the ice-cream vendor came pushing his wagon with a freezer chest holding so many treats! My favorite was a frozen Milky Way bar.

Some peddlers came every day or once in a while, but others had a schedule. The truck from the bakery came every other day. Wednesday was my favorite day. That's when the bakery delivered cupcakes with cream inside and chocolate frosting.

Peddlers rolled fruit and vegetable wagons down our street. "Watermelon for sale! Nice, cold watermelon!" they would yell.

I remember when a photographer came

down our street with a pony on a beautiful summer day. All the neighborhood children ran over to pet the pony, and the photographer let my sister and me ride it. Our parents thought we looked so cute on the pony that they had to have our photograph taken.

Home Deliveries

In those days, you could have your local grocery store deliver to your home. Some of my friends' mothers would call the grocery store with an order, and a delivery boy would bring it over the same day. They would pay for the goods when they received them, or the store would bill them later.

Sometimes my mom would call a department store and have something delivered or order things from a mail-order catalog — a few pairs of stockings or maybe a dress. It was always exciting to see the delivery man drive up in his truck and drop off a package. Maybe it was something special for my sister or me.

Milk was also delivered every other day; we didn't buy it in paper cartons at the store. In the winter, we made sure we got the glass bottles inside the house before the milk froze. Otherwise, the cream floating on top of the milk would pop the lids off the bottles. I loved licking the frozen cream. I tried not to let my mother catch me at it, though.

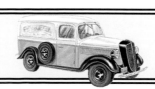

Stores Began to Change

As I got older, self-service supermarkets started to replace the individual shops in my neighborhood. This made for a huge change in the way we shopped. Instead of having store clerks get what we needed from shelves behind wooden counters, we walked down aisles of products, picking out the items we wanted. And there were so many more choices and different brands of the same food than before.

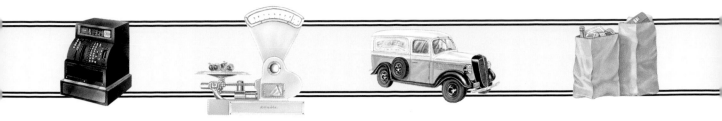

I couldn't buy just one cookie anymore, though. Instead of selling cookies in big bins, stores sold cookies packaged in cardboard boxes wrapped in cellophane.

Even though shopping has changed a lot since I was young, it's still just as exciting to visit stores and choose from so many wonderful things!

Glossary

cellophane: a thin, clear wrapping paper

cobbler: a person who makes and mends shoes

dry goods store: a store that sold clothing made in factories and material for people to sew their own clothes

duplex: a building that is divided into two homes, usually with a separate entrance for each home

icebox: a cabinet or box with a space for a large chunk of ice. The ice keeps the food inside the icebox cold. The ice melts into a pan beneath the icebox

nylon: a strong synthetic fabric used in clothing and to make parachutes

peddler: a person who travels around selling things

rationing: limiting to fixed portions. When certain items are scarce, sometimes the government limits, or rations, how many of those items people can buy.

streetcar: a vehicle for carrying people, powered by electric wires strung along a street. Unlike a bus, which looks similar, a streetcar runs along tracks set in the middle of a street.

tailor: a person who makes and mends clothes and alters them so they will fit

For Further Reading

Duden, Jane. *Timeline: 1940s.* New York: Crestwood House, 1989.

Milios, Rita. *Shopping Savvy.* New York: The Rosen Publishing Group, Inc., 1992.

Rubel, David. *The United States in the 20th Century.* New York: Scholastic Inc., 1995.

Van Rynbach, Iris. *Everything from a Nail to a Coffin.* New York: Orchard Books, 1991.

Whitman, Sylvia. *V Is for Victory: The American Home Front during World War II.* Minneapolis, Minn.: Lerner Publications Co., 1993.

Illustrations are reproduced through the courtesy of: Beverly Crawford, pp. 1, 4, 6, 7, 8, 25 (bottom), front cover (top left, bottom left), back cover (top); Milwaukee County Historical Society, pp. 5, 14 (top), 16, 17, 20, 21 (top), 22 (top), back cover (bottom); Corbis-Bettmann, pp. 9, 15, 19, 28; H. Armstrong Roberts, pp. 10, 11 (top), 12, 13, 25 (top); Stock Montage, p. 11 (bottom); Archive Photos/Lambert, p. 14, front cover (bottom right); FPG Intl., p. 18; Advertising Archives, pp. 21 (bottom), 22 (bottom left), 23; Brown Brothers, p. 24; UPI/Corbis-Bettmann, p. 26; Peter Newark's American Pictures, p. 27 (top); Archive Photos/Camerique, p. 27 (bottom); Corbis-Library of Congress, p. 29.

Index